Wonders

Reading/Writing Companion

Mc
Graw
Hill

mheducation.com/prek-12

Send all inquiries to:
McGraw Hill
1325 Avenue of the Americas
New York, NY 10019

ISBN: 978-1-26-574399-4
MHID: 1-26-574399-1

Printed in the United States of America.

2 3 4 5 6 7 8 9 LMN 26 25 24 23 22 21

A

Welcome to
WONDERS!

We're here to help you set goals to build on the amazing things you already know. We'll also help you reflect on everything you'll learn.

Let's start by taking a look at the incredible things you'll do this year.

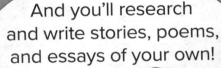

You'll build knowledge on exciting topics and find answers to interesting questions.

You'll read fascinating fiction, informational texts, and poetry and respond to what you read with your own thoughts and ideas.

And you'll research and write stories, poems, and essays of your own!

Here's a sneak peek at how you'll do it all.

"Let's go!"

You'll explore new ideas by reading groups of different texts about the same topic. These groups of texts are called *text sets*.

At the beginning of a text set, we'll help you set goals on the My Goals page. You'll see a bar with four boxes beneath each goal. Think about what you already know to fill in the bar. Here's an example.

I can read and understand realistic fiction.

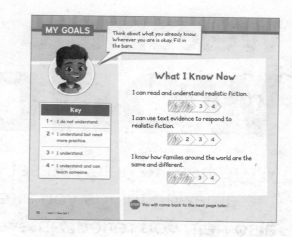

As you move through a text set, you'll explore an essential question and build your knowledge of a topic until you're ready to write about it yourself.

You'll also learn skills that will help you reach your text set goals. At the end of lessons, you'll see a new Check In bar with four boxes.

CHECK IN 〉 1 〉 2 〉 3 〉 4 〉

Reflect on how well you understood a lesson to fill in the bar.

Here are some questions you can ask yourself.

- Was I able to complete the task?

- Was it easy or was it hard?

- Do I think I need more practice?

You have plenty of tools and resources to learn more, such as anchor charts and center activities. You can also reread a lesson or ask a teacher or peer for help.

It's okay if I think I need more practice. The most important thing is that I do my best and keep learning!

Thinking about what works best for me helps me choose what to do next.

At the end of each text set, you'll show off the knowledge you built by completing a fun task. Then you'll return to the second My Goals page where we'll help you reflect on all that you learned.

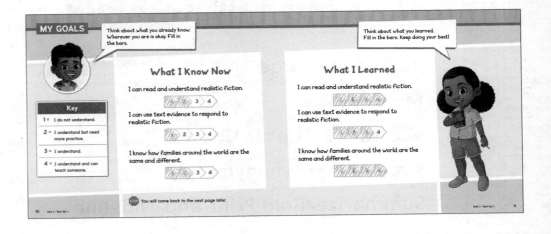

TEXT SET 1 **BIOGRAPHY**

TEXT SET 2 **REALISTIC FICTION**

TEXT SET 3 **OPINION TEXT**

GaryAlvis/E+/Getty Images

EXTENDED WRITING

CONNECT AND REFLECT

📖 Digital Tools

Find this eBook and other resources at **my.mheducation.com**

Build Knowledge

Essential Question

What do heroes do?

Build Vocabulary

Write new words you learned about what makes someone a hero. Draw lines and circles for the words you write.

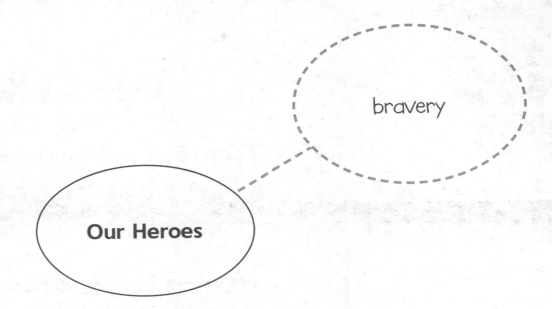

bravery

Our Heroes

BLAST BACK! studysync

Go online to **my.mheducation.com** and read the "What Makes a Hero?" Blast. Think about the qualities of a hero, or why we look up to heroes. Then blast back your response.

Think about what you already know. Fill in the bars. You'll learn more with practice.

What I Know Now

I can read and understand a biography.

1 > 2 > 3 > 4

I can use text evidence to respond to a biography.

1 > 2 > 3 > 4

I know about what heroes do.

1 > 2 > 3 > 4

Key	
1 =	I do not understand.
2 =	I understand but need more practice.
3 =	I understand.
4 =	I understand and can teach someone.

STOP You will come back to the next page later.

Think about what you learned. Fill in the bars. What is getting easier for you?

What I Learned

I can read and understand a biography.

1 > 2 > 3 > 4

I can use text evidence to respond to a biography.

1 > 2 > 3 > 4

I know about what heroes do.

1 > 2 > 3 > 4

My Goal I can read and understand a biography.

TAKE NOTES

As you read, write down interesting words and important information.

_____

_____

_____

_____

_____

_____

_____

_____

Cesar Chavez

Essential Question

?

What do heroes do?

Read about a man who took action to improve the lives of others.

Who are your **heroes?** For many farm workers, Cesar Chavez is a hero. He is the brave man who spent his life helping them.

Childhood

Cesar Chavez was born in Arizona. His parents taught him about learning, hard work, and respect.

Cesar worked on the family farm as a young boy. He helped care for the farm animals. His mother and grandmother taught Cesar about caring. Many people came to their door asking for food, and his kind family always shared.

Cesar had a strong **interest** in education. This desire to learn was sometimes hard on him. Spanish was his first language, but he needed to learn and **study** English. At school, he was punished for speaking Spanish.

His mother taught Cesar to find peaceful ways to solve problems. These lessons helped him **succeed** later in life. He would win struggles without fighting.

Siede Preis/Photodisc/Getty Images

FIND TEXT EVIDENCE

Read
Paragraphs 2–3
Summarize
Circle what Cesar Chavez's family taught him about. Summarize how he learned about caring for others.

_____

_____

_____

Paragraph 5
Author's Purpose
Draw a box around what Cesar's mother taught him. **Underline** how this helped him succeed later in life.

Reread
Author's Craft

How does the author get you interested in the biography in the first paragraph?

FIND TEXT EVIDENCE

Read

Paragraphs 1–2
Boldprint and Timeline
Underline what the drought caused. **Circle** two reasons why the family moved. **Circle** this event on the timeline.

Paragraph 3
Author's Purpose
Draw a box around what the family discovered in California. What does the author describe about farm workers?

_____

_____

_____

Reread

Author's Craft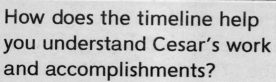

How does the timeline help you understand Cesar's work and accomplishments?

Hard Times

When Cesar was ten, it did not rain for a long time. This **drought** caused the plants on the farm to die. Without **crops** to sell, Cesar's family couldn't afford to keep the farm.

Then Cesar's family moved to California where there was no drought. His family traveled from farm to farm and worked the crops.

Cesar and his family would quickly **discover** that migrant farm workers had difficult lives. Their **challenging** jobs forced them to work long hours for little money. The workers bent over all day tending the crops. The work they had to **perform** made their backs hurt and their fingers bleed. If workers complained, farm owners fired them.

Timeline of Cesar Chavez's Life

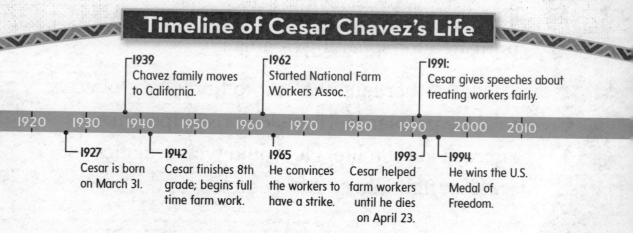

1939
Chavez family moves to California.

1962
Started National Farm Workers Assoc.

1991:
Cesar gives speeches about treating workers fairly.

1920   1930   1940   1950   1960   1970   1980   1990   2000   2010

1927
Cesar is born on March 31.

1942
Cesar finishes 8th grade; begins full time farm work.

1965
He convinces the workers to have a strike.

1993
Cesar helped farm workers until he dies on April 23.

1994
He wins the U.S. Medal of Freedom.

Changing Lives

Cesar knew the migrant workers were not treated fairly so he decided to take action. He told the migrant workers he had a plan.

It was time for grapes to be harvested, or picked. Cesar told the workers to stop working. This was called a **strike**. The grapes began to rot. With no grapes to sell, the landowners lost money. Finally, the owners talked to Cesar. They promised better pay. After that, the workers began picking the crops again.

Cesar Chavez worked for the rest of his life to improve farm workers' lives. Would you **agree** that he is a hero?

Retell

Use your notes and think about the details and ideas in "Cesar Chavez." Retell the events in the text.

Siede Preis/Photodisc/Getty Images

FIND TEXT EVIDENCE

Read
Paragraph 2
Synonyms
Draw a box around a synonym for *harvested*. When did Cesar tell workers to stop working?

_____

_____

_____

Author's Purpose
Underline what happened when the landowners lost money. **Circle** what happened after that.

Reread
Author's Craft

Why does the author ask a question at the conclusion, or end, of the biography?

Vocabulary

**Talk with a partner about each word.
Then answer the questions.**

agree

My friend and I **agree** to share the ball.

What is something you and a friend agree about?

_____

_____

challenging

This math problem is **challenging** to me.

Tell about something that is challenging for you
to do.

_____

_____

discover

I **discover** fun books to read at school.

What are some things you want to discover?

_____

_____

_____

heroes

Firefighters are **heroes** that help others.

What other people are heroes?

_____

interest

Adam has an **interest** in music.

Tell about an interest of yours.

_____

_____

Build Your Word List On page 15,
find three different words that
have the base word *work*. Use a word
web to write the words you found.

perform

My class likes to **perform** songs at school.

Tell about a time you saw someone perform.

_____

_____

study

I like to **study** the planets.

What do you like to study?

_____

_____

succeed

I hope I **succeed** in winning the game.

What do you do if you do not succeed at something at first?

_____

_____

Synonyms

Synonyms are words that have almost the same meaning. _Mad_ and _angry_ are synonyms. A synonym can be a clue to the meaning of a difficult word.

FIND TEXT EVIDENCE

On page 13 of "Cesar Chavez," I read the word caring. _In the last sentence of the same paragraph, I read the word_ kind. Caring _and_ kind _are synonyms._

His mother and grandmother taught Cesar about caring. Many people came to their door asking for food, and his kind family always shared.

Your Turn Find a synonym in the text for the word below.

problems, page 13 _____

Write a sentence using a pair of synonyms.

CHECK IN   1   2   3   4

Summarize

Summarizing is using your own words to tell the most important details. This can help you remember information.

🔍 **FIND TEXT EVIDENCE**

After reading page 15 of "Cesar Chavez," I can summarize what Cesar did to help farm workers.

Page 15

It was time for the grapes to be harvested, or picked. Cesar told the workers to stop working. This was called a **strike**. The grapes began to rot. With no grapes to sell, the landowners lost money. Finally, the owners talked to Cesar. They promised better pay. After that, the workers began picking the crops again.

I read that Cesar talked to other farm workers and they had a strike. When the owners promised better pay, the strike ended.

Your Turn Summarize the section "Childhood" on page 13.

_____

_____

_____

CHECK IN 1 2 3 4

Bold Print and Timeline

"Cesar Chavez" is a biography. It is a true story of a person's life that is written by another person. The author uses text features, such as words in bold print and a timeline.

 FIND TEXT EVIDENCE

I can tell that "Cesar Chavez" is a biography because it tells about the life of Cesar Chavez. Another clue is that it has a timeline of his life and important words in bold print.

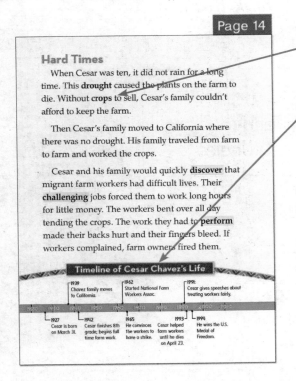

Page 14

Hard Times

When Cesar was ten, it did not rain for a long time. This **drought** caused the plants on the farm to die. Without **crops** to sell, Cesar's family couldn't afford to keep the farm.

Then Cesar's family moved to California where there was no drought. His family traveled from farm to farm and worked the crops.

Cesar and his family would quickly **discover** that migrant farm workers had difficult lives. Their **challenging** jobs forced them to work long hours for little money. The workers bent over all day tending the crops. The work they had to **perform** made their backs hurt and their fingers bleed. If workers complained, farm owners fired them.

Bold print shows words that are important to understand the topic.

A **timeline** shows dates of events in the order that they happened.

 Your Turn How does the author use the timeline to add details to the biography?

Author's Purpose

An author has a purpose, or reason, for writing. An author writes a biography to inform readers about important and interesting things about a person's life. Some authors use time order to show how events in the text are connected.

FIND TEXT EVIDENCE

As I read page 13 of "Cesar Chavez," I learn young Cesar was taught lessons on a farm in Arizona. His mother taught him to find peaceful ways to solve problems. I think this is a clue to the author's purpose.

> **First**
>
> Cesar was born on a farm in Arizona. He learned from his mother to find peaceful ways to win struggles.

Your Turn Reread "Cesar Chavez." Fill in the graphic organizer with more clues. Then use the graphic organizer to explain the author's purpose.

CHECK IN 1 2 3 4

First

Cesar Chavez was born on a farm in Arizona. He learned from his mother to find peaceful ways to win struggles.

↓

Next

↓

Then

↓

Last

Respond to Reading

COLLABORATE

Discuss the prompt below. Use your notes and text evidence to support your response.

What did Cesar Chavez learn as a boy that helped him become a hero when he grew up?

_____

_____

_____

_____

_____

_____

_____

_____

_____

Quick Tip

Use these sentence starters to help you organize your text evidence.

Cesar learned...

Cesar Chavez wanted to help...

Grammar Connections

Always capitalize proper nouns, such as the names of people and states:

Cesar Chavez *and his family moved to* ***California***.

CHECK IN 1 2 3 4

American Hero

Follow the research process to create a poster of an American hero, such as Amelia Earhart or Sojourner Truth. Work with a partner.

Step 1 **Set a Goal** Decide on an American hero. Think about what you know about this person's life and what you want to find out.

Write your topic: _____

_____

Step 2 **Identify Sources** Relevant sources of information can be books, magazine articles, or websites.

Step 3 **Find and Record Information** Retell in your own words information you want to show. Paraphrasing will help you better understand facts and ideas. Cite your sources of information.

Step 4 **Organize and Combine Information** Group information that tells about the same ideas or events. You may organize important events in sequence, or in the order they happened.

Look away from a source when you take notes. This will help you write down ideas in your own words.

Step 5 **Create and Present** Create the poster that tells why the person is important to American history. Take turns presenting your poster to the class.

JGI/Jamie Grill/Blend Images LLC

CHECK IN 1 > 2 > 3 > 4 >

Brave Bessie

? Why does the author begin the biography by telling about the library wagon?

Literature Anthology: pages 390–401

 Talk About It Reread page 391. Discuss how Bessie feels about the books from the library wagon.

Cite Text Evidence Write details that tell why the library wagon was important to Bessie. Then write how the details help you understand what Bessie did later.

Quick Tip

As you reread, think about how the author connects ideas from the beginning to the end of Bessie's biography.

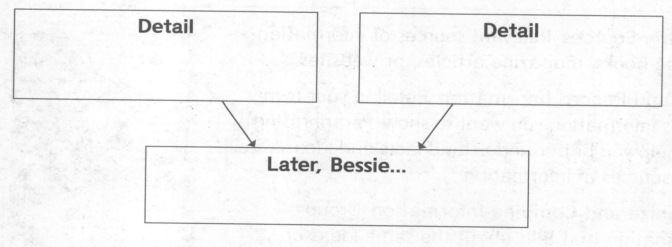

Detail	Detail

Later, Bessie...

 Make Inferences

Talk with a partner about the illustration. What inference can you make about when Bessie grew up from evidence in the text and illustration?

Write The author begins by telling about the library

wagon because _____

_____

CHECK IN 1 2 3 4

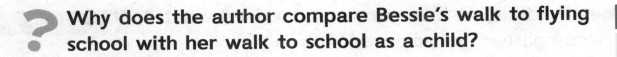 **Why does the author compare Bessie's walk to flying school with her walk to school as a child?**

COLLABORATE

Talk About It Reread paragraph 1 on page 392 and paragraph 3 on page 396. What did Bessie do each day?

Text Evidence Take notes on the paragraphs. Then tell what the details both show.

In Texas, Bessie...	These details both show...
In France, Bessie...	

Write The author compares Bessie's two walks to _____

_____

_____

Quick Tip

Use these sentence starters to help you explain why Besssie walked so far.

Bessie knew school was...

Bessie had to walk...

Bessie practiced...

Combine Information

Think about what Bessie had needed to do to get to France and what she did in France. What do these details all show?

CHECK IN 1 2 3 4

? How does the timeline help you to understand what Bessie accomplished, or achieved?

Talk About It Reread the timeline on page 398. Talk about the important events that it shows.

Cite Text Evidence Write details from the selection for three of Bessie's accomplishments on the timeline.

Year	Event

Write The timeline helps me understand Bessie's accomplishments because _____

_____

_____

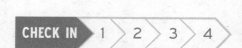

CHECK IN   1   2   3   4

Respond to Reading

COLLABORATE

Discuss the prompt below. Use your notes and text evidence to support your response.

How does Bessie's story show what it means to be a hero?

_____

_____

_____

_____

_____

_____

_____

_____

Quick Tip

Use these sentence starters to organize your text evidence.

When Bessie was a girl...

Bessie needed to...

She wanted people to see...

CHECK IN 1 2 3 4

The Prince's Frog

Literature Anthology: pages 402-405

The Queen noticed her son's disappointment. "Take good care of your royal pet," she told him. "Make sure that your frog has everything a frog needs to be healthy and happy." Peter felt glum, but he did as he was told. He put the frog in a dish of water. He captured flies and fed his pet. *Snap, gulp!* The frog's sticky tongue darted out and swallowed hungrily. "Yuck!" Peter thought.

Reread the text. **Underline** what the Queen tells her son to do. **Circle** words that describe how Peter feels.

Draw a box around the description of the frog eating. Why does Peter think "Yuck!" when he watches the frog?

_____

_____

_____

COLLABORATE

How does the author help you understand that it is difficult for Peter to take care of his new pet frog?

For three days, the Queen watched as Peter's interest in the frog grew. She was happy to see her son and his pet splash and laugh in the royal pool. Peter always made sure the frog was safe and had everything a frog needs to be healthy and happy. The Queen was pleased to see her son take good care of his pet.

On the third night, the frog told the prince, "I feel lucky to be your pet."

Peter felt lucky, too. A prince could never wish for a better pet then his friendly frog. He kissed the frog on its slimy head. "I will always take care of you, my friend."

Reread paragraph 1. **Underline** why the Queen is happy. What details in the text and illustration show Peter is having fun with his pet?

_____

_____

_____

Circle what Peter does for his pet. **Draw a box** around what the Queen is pleased to see.

COLLABORATE

Discuss how the author describes the Queen's feelings as a way to tell you about Peter.

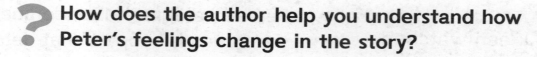

? **How does the author help you understand how Peter's feelings change in the story?**

Talk About It Reread pages 28 and 29. Talk about details that show how Peter feels about his pet.

Cite Text Evidence Write details about the character Peter. Then tell how his feelings change in the story.

Details	How Peter Changes

Write The author helps me understand how _____

_____

_____

> ### Quick Tip
>
> Story characters may change as they learn an important lesson. Peter's feelings about his pet frog change in the story. Think about what he has learned by the end.

CHECK IN 1 2 3 4

Character Perspective

The narrator of "The Prince's Frog" is not a character. The fairy tale is told from the third-person point of view. The narrator describes the different perspectives, or attitudes, of the characters throughout the story.

FIND TEXT EVIDENCE

On page 28, The narrator describes Peter's feelings of disappointment about his pet. The Queen's dialogue shows that she has a different attitude from her son.

> The Queen noticed her son's disappointment. "Take good care of your royal pet," she told him.

Your Turn Look back at details on page 29. Explain the perspectives, or attitudes, of the Queen and Peter at the end of the story.

_____

_____

_____

Quick Tip

The author uses pronouns such as *he* or *she* to tell what different characters think or feel about events in a story.

CHECK IN 1 2 3 4

? **What have you learned about what heroes do from the selections and the statue of Paul Revere?**

COLLABORATE

Talk About It Look at the photograph and read the caption. Talk with a partner about what you know about Paul Revere. Why do you think he is a hero?

Cite Text Evidence **Circle** the detail in the caption that tells why the statue has been built. **Underline** why people think Paul Revere is a hero.

Write The selections I read and this photograph

help me understand that heroes are _____

_____

_____

_____

_____

_____

_____

The sculpture honors Paul Revere's famous Midnight Ride. He risked his life to help protect the safety of others.

CHECK IN ❯ 1 ❯ 2 ❯ 3 ❯ 4

brians10/iStock/Getty Images

Write an Inspirational Speech

Think about the people in the texts you read. Think about the challenges they faced and their achievements. How do heroes inspire others to do their best?

1 Look at your Build Knowledge notes in your reader's notebook.

2 Write a speech that explains how heroes you read about inspire you. Describe three heroes who you admire. Explain why you want to be like these heroes.

3 Include some of the new words you learned. Be sure to use examples from three of the texts you read in your speech.

Think about what you learned in this text set. Fill in the bars on page 11.

Build Knowledge

? Essential Question

What do good citizens do?

Build Vocabulary

 Write new words you learned about what good citizens do. Draw lines and circles for the words you write.

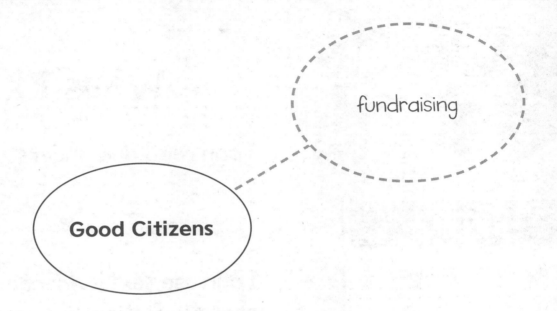

fundraising

Good Citizens

 Go online to **my.mheducation.com** and read the "I Can Be a Good Citizen, Too" Blast. Think about how people act as good citizens. Then blast back your response.

Think about what you already know. Fill in the bars. Keep doing your best!

What I Know Now

I can read and understand realistic fiction.

| 1 | 2 | 3 | 4 |

I can use text evidence to respond to realistic fiction.

| 1 | 2 | 3 | 4 |

I know about what good citizens do.

| 1 | 2 | 3 | 4 |

Key

1 =	I do not understand.
2 =	I understand but need more practice.
3 =	I understand.
4 =	I understand and can teach someone.

STOP You will come back to the next page later.

> Think about what you learned. Fill in the bars. You can always improve so keep trying!

What I Learned

I can read and understand realistic fiction.

1 2 3 4

I can use text evidence to respond to realistic fiction.

1 2 3 4

I know about what good citizens do.

1 2 3 4

My Goal I can read and understand realistic fiction.

TAKE NOTES

As you read, write down interesting words and important events.

_____

_____

_____

_____

_____

_____

_____

_____

A Difficult Decision

Essential Question

?

What do good citizens do?

Read about a boy who chooses to be a good citizen.

My best friend Paul and I were excited to go to the park after school. The park had a new fort. The Parks Department let the kids choose what kind of equipment to build, and the fort got the most **votes.** After school, Mom and I met Paul and his dad at the park.

Paul and I raced to the top of the tower. "I win. I'm the **champion,**" I shouted. "Look, Paul! Someone left the newest GameMaster here. It's mine now!"

Paul raised his eyebrows and looked thoughtful. "Wyatt, you cannot keep that GameMaster," he said. "You have a **responsibility** to return it. It is your duty!"

I asked, "Haven't you ever heard the saying, 'finders keepers, losers weepers'? I have **rights.** I found it, so I am claiming it."

FIND TEXT EVIDENCE

Read

Paragraphs 1 and 2

Plot: Beginning, Middle, End

Circle what the narrator finds in the park. **Draw a box** around what he says about it.

Paragraph 3

Character Perspective

Underline the sentences that explain Paul's perspective about the GameMaster. What does Paul think Wyatt should do?

_____

_____

Reread

Author's Craft

How does the author use dialogue to show that the characters feel differently?

SHARED READ

FIND TEXT EVIDENCE

Read

▼ Paragraph 3

Make and Confirm Predictions

Underline the sentence that helps you make a prediction about what Wyatt will do with the GameMaster. Why does he decide to do this?

_____

_____

Paragraph 4

Character Perspective

Draw a box around the word that shows Paul thinks Wyatt made a good decision.

Reread
Author's Craft

How does the author use Paul's dialogue to help you understand Wyatt's traits?

"You can do whatever you want, Wyatt, but you know it's wrong to keep it," Paul said. Then he added, "Whenever there are **issues** like this at school, you're the one who helps solve the problems. Now you aren't taking your own advice."

Then Paul added, "I **volunteered** my thoughts. If you don't want to take the help I offered, there's nothing I can do."

Paul was right. I couldn't keep the game because it wasn't mine. The person who lost it would be upset. I cleared my throat and said in my best deep voice, "I've **determined** that you're right!"

"I'm delighted you decided to do the right thing," said Paul.

We told my mother what happened. She walked around the park with us so we could try to find the owner of the game. Soon we saw a boy and his Mom looking for something. He looked hopeless, and he burst into tears when we asked him if the game was his. "Yes," he wailed, "I lost my GameMaster a little while ago. I should have been more careful!"

Afterward, Mom and I walked home. I was glad I returned the toy to the boy. So, I made a **promise** to myself to always try to do the right thing. Now that is a vow I can keep!

Retell

Use your notes and think about what happens in "A Difficult Decision." Retell the most important events in the story.

FIND TEXT EVIDENCE

Read

Paragraph 1
Suffixes

Underline the word that means "without hope." **Circle** the word ending.

Paragraph 1
Make and Confirm Predictions

Confirm your prediction on page 40. How was it right?

_____

_____

_____

Reread
Author's Craft

Why does the author include a description of the boy who lost the GameMaster?

Vocabulary

**Talk with a partner about each word.
Then answer the questions.**

champion

Maya won the game and became the
new **champion**.

What would you get if you were the champion of
a game?

_____

_____

determined

The boy **determined** which books to check
out at the library.

Who determined what you will read today?

_____

_____

issues

The teachers met to talk about important
school **issues**.

What are some important issues in your school?

_____

_____

promises

Zack and Jon made a **promise** to tell the
truth.

Why should you keep your promise?

_____

_____

responsibility

It is my **responsibility** to clean my room.

What is a responsibility you have at home?

_____

_____

Build Your Word List Pick a word
from the story. Use a thesaurus to look
up synonyms and antonyms of the word.

rights

Going to school is one of your **rights** as a citizen.

What rights do you have?

_____

_____

volunteered

I **volunteered** to pick up trash in our park.

When is a time you volunteered to help?

_____

_____

votes

The teacher counted the **votes** for the class president.

Why do we use votes to decide things?

_____

_____

Suffixes

To figure out a word's meaning, separate the base word from its suffix, such as: care • less, help • ful, sharp • er, clean • est, select • ion.

🔍 FIND TEXT EVIDENCE

I'm not sure what thoughtful _means. Its base word_ thought _has to do with thinking. Its suffix_ –ful _means "full of." Thoughtful may mean "having a lot of thoughts."_

Paul raised his eyebrows and looked thoughtful.

Your Turn Use suffixes to figure out the meanings of the words from page 41.

owner _____

careful _____

CHECK IN 1 2 3 4

Daniel Griffo

Make and Confirm Predictions

Use what you know about realistic fiction to help you predict, or guess, what might happen next. As you read, check to see if your predictions are correct.

🔍 **FIND TEXT EVIDENCE**

As you read page 40, use the realistic dialogue between the two boys to make a prediction about what Paul will say next.

Page 40

> Then Paul added, "I **volunteered** my thoughts. If you don't want to take the help I offered, there's nothing I can do."

I predict that Paul will say the right things to convince Wyatt to return the GameMaster.

Your Turn When Wyatt saw the sad boy, what did you predict would happen? Confirm if your prediction is correct.

_____

_____

_____

CHECK IN 1 2 3 4

Plot: Beginning, Middle, End

"A Difficult Decision" is realistic fiction. Realistic fiction has characters, a setting, and events that could really happen. It often has a beginning, middle, and end.

When you write realistic fiction, ask yourself: *Does the dialogue sound like real people talking? Would people act this way if the event really happened?*

🔍 FIND TEXT EVIDENCE

I can tell that "A Difficult Decision" is realistic fiction. Wyatt and Paul act like real people. The story has three clear parts that help me follow events and understand the characters.

Page 39

My best friend Paul and I were excited to go to the park after school. The park had a new fort. The Parks Department let the kids choose what kind of equipment to build, and the fort got the most **votes.** After school, Mom and I met Paul and his dad at the park.

Paul and I raced to the top of the tower. "I win. I'm the **champion,**" I shouted. "Look, Paul! Someone left the newest GameMaster here. It's mine now!"

Paul raised his eyebrows and looked thoughtful. "Wyatt, you cannot keep that GameMaster," he said. "You have a **responsibility** to return it. It is your duty!"

I asked, "Haven't you ever heard the saying, 'finders keepers, losers weepers'? I have **rights.** I found it, so I am claiming it."

Beginning, Middle, End
In the beginning of the story, the characters go to the park after school. Wyatt finds a game and wants to keep it.

Your Turn How do Wyatt's feelings change about the game he finds in different parts of the story?

_____

_____

_____

Character Perspective

A character telling the story has a perspective, or feelings, about story events. Dialogue and descriptions of what other characters do can show different characters' perspectives.

🔍 FIND TEXT EVIDENCE

When I read the second paragraph on page 39 of "A Difficult Decision," I can tell Wyatt is talking. I will look for clues to his perspective on finding the game.

Character	Clue	Perspective
Wyatt	"It's mine, now!"	Wyatt thinks he should keep a game he found.

Quick Tip

A character in the story, Wyatt, is the narrator. This is called first-person point of you. Look for clues in what other characters say for their perspectives on events.

COLLABORATE

Your Turn Continue rereading the story. Identify clues to the perspectives of Wyatt and Paul on the game that Wyatt finds. Fill in the graphic organizer.

CHECK IN 1 2 3 4

Daniel Griffo

Character	Clues	Perspective
Wyatt	"It's mine, now!"	Wyatt thinks he should keep a game he found.

Respond to Reading

COLLABORATE Talk about the prompt below. Use your notes and text evidence to support your ideas.

How does Wyatt learn to be a better citizen?

_____

_____

_____

_____

_____

_____

_____

_____

_____

Quick Tip

Use these sentence starters to help you organize your text evidence.

Wyatt believes...

Paul tells him...

Wyatt understands...

Grammar Connections

Proper nouns are capitalized, no matter where they are in a sentence. Proper nouns include names of people, certain places, days of the week, and holidays.

CHECK IN　1　2　3　4

Government Leader

COLLABORATE

With a partner, create a pamphlet describing why you would be a good mayor, governor, or president. Follow the research process to create your pamphlet.

Step 1 **Set a Goal** Decide on a government role to research.

Write your topic: _____

Step 2 **Identify Sources** Relevant sources can be books, magazine articles, or websites.

Step 3 **Find and Record Information** Write questions about the topic. Then research and record the answers. Take notes in your own words.

Write two questions: _____

_____

_____

Step 4 **Organize and Combine Information** Organize information that supports reasons you would make a positive contribution to the community.

The capital city of Florida is Tallahassee.

Step 5 **Create and Present** Create the final pamphlet. Share why you would be a good mayor, governor, or president. Be sure to explain what you could do for people and the community.

Ilene MacDonald/Alamy Stock Photo

CHECK IN 〉 1 〉 2 〉 3 〉 4 〉

Grace for President

? **How does the author use illustrations to help you predict what will happen next?**

Literature Anthology: pages 406–427

Talk About It Reread page 408. Talk about what Grace says and what is on the wall behind her.

Cite Text Evidence Write clues from the text and the illustration. Then write how they show what will happen next.

Clue from Text

What happens next?

Clue from Illustration

Write The author uses illustrations to help you predict

_____

_____

CHECK IN ⟩ 1 ⟩ 2 ⟩ 3 ⟩ 4 ⟩

? **What does the author's placement of the illustrations show you about the campaigns?**

Talk About It Reread pages 413–415. Talk about how the illustrations are placed and what they show.

Cite Text Evidence Write details about Grace's campaign, Thomas's campaign, and both campaigns.

Grace's Campaign   Both Campaigns   Thomas's Campaign

Write The author places the illustrations to show

_____

_____

_____

CHECK IN ▷ 1 ▷ 2 ▷ 3 ▷ 4 ▷

? **Why does the author end the page with only one state's votes unaccounted for?**

Talk About It Reread pages 421–422. Talk about how the author ends page 422.

Cite Text Evidence In the circles below, write three reasons the author ends the page with Wyoming.

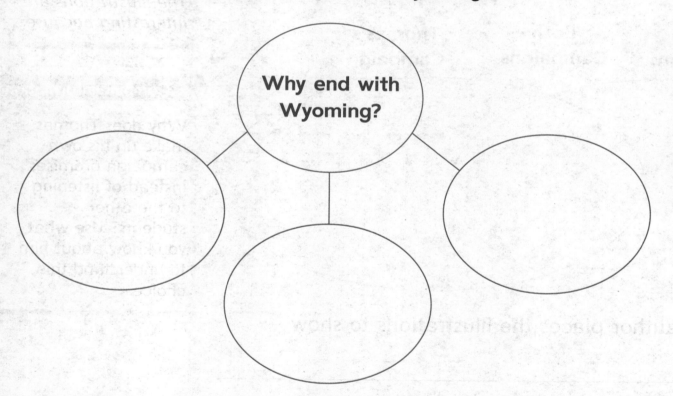

Why end with Wyoming?

Write The author ends the page this way to _____

_____

CHECK IN 1 2 3 4

Respond to Reading

Discuss the prompt below. Use your notes and text evidence to support your opinion.

What is your opinion about who will make a better president in the story?

_____

_____

_____

_____

_____

_____

_____

_____

My Goal I can use text evidence to respond to realistic fiction.

Quick Tip

Use these sentence starters to help you organize your text evidence.

Grace makes promises after…

Thomas wants…

Grace continues her campaign…

Soon before the election,…

Helping to Make Smiles

Literature Anthology:
pages 428–429

Camp Smiles

During the summer, Matthew goes to Camp Smiles. It is an Easter Seals camp for children with disabilities. Children with special needs often can't go to other camps. Other camps cannot help them meet their needs. At Camp Smiles there is special gear. Each camper has a buddy to help him or her. Children at Camp Smiles are able to ride horses, play basketball, and swim. Camp may be the only place where they can do those activities.

Reread the paragraph. **Underline** the sentence with information the author gives about Camp Smiles and the campers who go there.

Circle what campers can do at Camp Smiles.

COLLABORATE

Discuss why Camp Smiles is a special place. Write evidence from the paragraph that supports your answer.

_____

_____

_____

_____

Matthew's Camp Challenge

Matthew had a great time at Camp Smiles. He wanted other kids like him to go to camp. Not all kids can afford to go to camp. Matthew wanted to change that. He decided to challenge people to give money. The money will pay for 30 children to go to Camp Smiles. Matthew showed responsibility. He is involved in his community. He is helping to make children with disabilities smile.

Reread the paragraph. **Underline** two ways Matthew is a good citizen. Explain them here.

_____

_____

Circle how Matthew helped pay for more kids to go to camp.

COLLABORATE

With a partner, discuss what *community* means in this selection. What communities is Matthew involved with? Write your answer here.

_____

_____

_____

_____

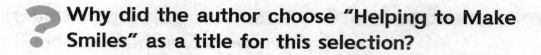

? **Why did the author choose "Helping to Make Smiles" as a title for this selection?**

As you reread to answer questions, look for examples in the text to support your answers.

COLLABORATE

Talk About It Talk about the different ways people in the community help children with disabilities.

Cite Text Evidence Write about the different people who bring smiles to the campers and how those people help.

People	How They Help

Write The author chose the title name because

_____

_____

_____

_____

CHECK IN ▷ 1 ⟩ 2 ⟩ 3 ⟩ 4 ⟩

Graphic Features and Callouts

A callout is a short piece of text that has larger type or different type. Authors use graphic features such as callouts to give more information about a topic.

FIND TEXT EVIDENCE

Reread the callout on page 429. Think about why the author uses a callout for this information. Answer the questions below.

What is the title of the callout? _____

What makes someone a good citizen?

- _____ - _____

- _____ - _____

Your Turn Why do you think the author put this information in a callout?

_____

_____

_____

Quick Tip

As you read nonfiction such as "Helping to Make Smiles," look for information in the text and graphic features. Authors can use callouts to share information not found in the main part of the text. Think about what this information adds to the topic.

CHECK IN 1 2 3 4

Integrate **MAKE CONNECTIONS**

? **What have you learned from the selections you read and the song "America the Beautiful" about being a good citizen?**

Talk About It Discuss what it means for a citizen to sing the song "America the Beautiful."

Cite Text Evidence **Circle** details in the song that help you understand what is beautiful about America. Talk about what good citizens do to keep America beautiful.

Write Stories and songs like "America the Beautiful" show us

_____

_____

Quick Tip

When you read, it helps to think about how you can make connections between texts. You can ask yourself: *How are the ideas in the texts similar and different?*

America the Beautiful

O beautiful for spacious skies,
For amber waves of grain.
For purple mountain majesties,
Above the fruited plain.
America! America!

God shed His grace on thee,
And crown thy good with brotherhood,
From sea to shining sea.

— Music by Samuel Ward
— Words by Katharine Lee Bates

CHECK IN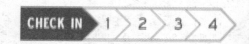

PHOTO:pbakerp/iStock/Getty Images; TEXT: Jackson, Henry E. (Special Agent in Community Organization United States Bureau of Education) and Von Slyck, Clara L. (Formerly with Department of Recreation Russell Sage Foundation), Liberty Day: October 12, 1918: Suggestions for Community Celebrations. Washington, 1918.

58 Unit 5 · Text Set 2

I know about what good citizens do.

Give Advice to Second Graders

Think about the characters and real-life people you read about. Think about how their actions make them good citizens. How do they show kids how to be a good citizen?

1. Look at your Build Knowledge notes in your reader's notebook.

2. Create a pamphlet that explains how a second grader can be a good citizen. In your pamphlet, use examples from the texts you read to support your ideas. You may also describe how you try to be a good citizen.

3. Include some of the new words you learned. Remember to use evidence from three texts to support your ideas.

Think about what you learned in this text set. Fill in the bars on page 37.

Build Knowledge

? Essential Question

Why are rules important?

Build Vocabulary

Write new words you learned about why rules are important. Draw lines and circles for the words you write.

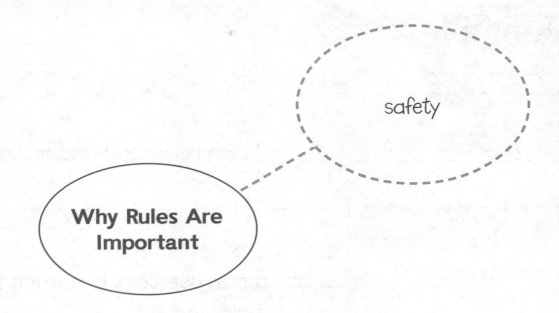

safety

Why Rules Are Important

Go online to **my.mheducation.com** and read the "Rules of Respect at School" Blast. Think about why we need rules at school. Then blast back your response.

Think about what you already know. Fill in the bars. We all do better with practice.

Key

1 =	I do not understand.
2 =	I understand but need more practice.
3 =	I understand.
4 =	I understand and can teach someone.

What I Know Now

I can read and understand opinion text.

1 > 2 > 3 > 4

I can use text evidence to respond to opinion text.

1 > 2 > 3 > 4

I know about why rules are important.

1 > 2 > 3 > 4

 You will come back to the next page later.

Think about what you learned.
Fill in the bars. Good job!

What I Learned

I can read and understand opinion text.

| 1 | 2 | 3 | 4 |

I can use text evidence to respond to opinion text.

| 1 | 2 | 3 | 4 |

I know about why rules are important.

| 1 | 2 | 3 | 4 |

My Goal I can read and understand opinion text.

TAKE NOTES

As you read, write down interesting words and important information.

TIME for KiDS

The Problem with PLASTIC BAGS

Essential Question

? **Why are rules important?**

Read about whether there should be rules for recycling plastic bags.

For most Americans, plastic bags are part of shopping. Often these bags get thrown away soon after the trip to the store. About 500 billion bags are produced each year around the world. Fewer than 3% are recycled. This has a serious impact on the environment.

Some U.S. cities have created **rules** that ban plastic bags in stores. But not everyone is **united** behind these laws. People argue that we can continue to use plastic bags and still have the ability to protect the planet.

FIND TEXT EVIDENCE

Read

Paragraph 1
Multiple-Meaning Words
Circle the words that help you understand what "trip" means.

Paragraph 2
Summarize
Underline how some cities are dealing with plastic bags. Summarize how people feel about this issue.

_____

_____

_____

Reread
Author's Craft

Why does the author include facts with numbers about plastic bags?

FIND TEXT EVIDENCE

Read

Paragraph 1

Evaluate Information

Why did the number of bags littering the streets of California drop? **Draw a box** around the sentence that helps you explain this.

Reread

Author's Craft

What are two reasons the author states for a ban on using plastic bags?

TIME for **KiDS**

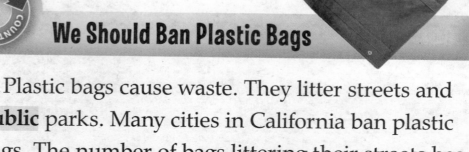

We Should Ban Plastic Bags

Plastic bags cause waste. They litter streets and **public** parks. Many cities in California ban plastic bags. The number of bags littering their streets has dropped.

Plastic bags pollute our land and water. This hurts wildlife. Some fish and birds can mistake the plastic for food. This may cause serious health problems and other dangers for the animals.

It takes resources to make plastic bags. We need to **finally** limit our use of plastic to save these resources. A ban will help shoppers **form** the habit of bringing reusable bags to stores.

We Still Need Plastic Bags

Let's look at **history** and learn from our mistakes. We don't need a ban. We need better ways to recycle. Many stores are now helping to make recycling easier. They put out bins for plastic bags. This limits litter and pollution. It also helps save Earth's resources.

Writers of laws to ban plastic bags do not understand how it hurts shoppers. Plastic bags are convenient. People cannot carry reusable bags at all times. It costs money to buy reusable bags. People have **exclaimed** they need those dollars to spend on their families.

Reasons to Ban Plastic Bags	Reasons to Keep Plastic Bags
Less waste and litter	Convenient to use
Protects animals	Can be recycled
Saves Earth's resources	Saves customers money

Retell

Use your notes and think about each opinion in "The Problem with Plastic Bags." Then retell each argument.

OPINION TEXT

FIND TEXT EVIDENCE

Read

Paragraph 2
Author's Purpose
Circle the two details that support how a ban would hurt shoppers. Why would a ban not be convenient?

_____

_____

Charts

Look at the chart. **Underline** a fact in each column that gives information about helping the planet.

Reread

Author's Craft

Why does the author use a chart to summarize two sides of the argument?

Vocabulary

Talk with a partner about each word. Then answer the questions.

exclaimed

"What a fun surprise!" James **exclaimed**.

How do you think James felt when he exclaimed about the surprise?

_____

_____

finally

Jen **finally** learned how to dive.

What is something that you finally learned how to do?

_____

_____

> **Build Your Word List** Reread paragraph 1 on page 65. Circle *shopping*. Use a word web to write other forms for this word.

form

Charlie and Amy want to **form** a chess club.

What kind of club would you like to form?

_____

_____

history

Ben learned about the **history** of his family.

What is something in history you want to learn about?

_____

_____

public

The park is Gina's favorite **public** place.

What public place do you like to visit?

_____

_____

_____

rules

We must follow the **rules** in the gym.

What is a a rule at your school?

_____

_____

united

The team **united** to win the game.

Why is it important for a team to be united?

_____

_____

writers

The **writers** finished their stories.

Name a famous writer who lived long ago.

_____

_____

Multiple-Meaning Words

You may find words that have more than one meaning. Rereading the sentence will help you figure out the correct meaning.

FIND TEXT EVIDENCE

On page 66, I see the word save. _I know that_ save _means "to help someone from danger." It can also mean "to keep something." When I read the sentence, the meaning "to keep something" makes sense._

We need to finally limit our use of plastic to save these resources.

Your Turn Write the correct meaning of each word from page 66 below, based on the sentence.

parks _____

land _____

CHECK IN ⟩ 1 ⟩ 2 ⟩ 3 ⟩ 4 ⟩

Summarize

When you summarize, you use your own words to retell the most important information in a text. Summarizing helps you understand what you read.

🔍 **FIND TEXT EVIDENCE**

After reading the first paragraph of "The Problem with Plastic Bags," I can summarize the important points.

Page 65

For most Americans, plastic bags are part of shopping. Often these bags get thrown away soon after the trip to the store. About 500 billion bags are produced each year around the world. Fewer than 3% are recycled. This has a serious impact on the environment.

People use billions of plastic bags every year. Few are recycled. This hurts the environment.

Your Turn Write a summary of paragraph 1 on page 67.

_____

_____

_____

CHECK IN ▷ 1 ▷ 2 ▷ 3 ▷ 4 ▷

Charts

"The Problem with Plastic Bags" is opinion text. It states an opinion about a topic. It has facts and examples to support the opinion. Opinion texts often include text features, such as charts.

Readers to Writers

Readers to Writers

When you write an opinion essay, think about how you can show information that supports your opinion in a chart.

🔍 FIND TEXT EVIDENCE

I can tell "The Problem with Plastic Bags" is opinion text. It gives facts and opinions. It uses facts and examples, or supporting evidence, to convince someone to think a certain way about a ban on plastic bags. The text also has a chart.

Page 67

We Still Need Plastic Bags

Let's look at **history** and learn from our mistakes. We don't need a ban. We need better ways to recycle. Many stores are now helping to make recycling easier. They put out bins for plastic bags. This limits litter and pollution. It also helps save Earth's resources.

Writers of laws to ban plastic bags do not understand how it hurts shoppers. Plastic bags are convenient. People cannot carry reusable bags at all times. It costs money to buy reusable bags. People have **exclaimed** they need those dollars to spend on their families.

Reasons to Ban Plastic Bags	Reasons to Keep Plastic Bags
Less waste and litter	Convenient to use
Protects animals	Can be recycled
Saves Earth's resources	Saves customers money

Retell

Use your notes and think about each opinion in "The Problem with Plastic Bags." Then retell each argument.

Chart

A chart is a list of information that is shown in rows. The heading tells that these facts explain why plastic bags should not be banned.

Your Turn Why does the author include a chart in the article?

_____

_____

_____

CHECK IN 1 2 3 4

Author's Purpose

Authors can write a text for different purposes, or reasons. A text can teach readers information or try to persuade the reader to think a certain way.

🔍 FIND TEXT EVIDENCE

As I reread page 66 of "The Problem with Plastic Bags," I identify the facts and examples. I see that cities that ban plastic bags have less litter now. I can use this fact as a clue to figure out the author's purpose for writing "We Should Ban Plastic Bags."

Clue

Litter has dropped in cities that ban plastic bags.

Your Turn Reread page 66. Fill in the graphic organizer to help you identify the author's purpose using clues found in the selection.

CHECK IN ⟩ 1 ⟩ 2 ⟩ 3 ⟩ 4

Clue

Litter has dropped in cities that ban plastic bags.

Clue

Clue

Author's Purpose

Respond to Reading

Talk about the prompt below. Use your notes and text evidence to support your opinion.

COLLABORATE

I can use text evidence to respond to opinion text.

What is your opinion about whether or not we should ban plastic bags?

_____

_____

_____

_____

_____

_____

_____

_____

Quick Tip

Use these sentence starters to help you organize your text evidence.

Plastic bags are/ are not a problem because...

The reasons are...

The supporting evidence is...

CHECK IN 1 2 3 4

Recycling

With a partner, create a recycling chart that answers the research question: *What items in your home can be recycled?* Follow the research process to create your chart.

Step 1 **Set a Goal** Decide on key words you will use to conduct online research.

Write key words: _____

_____

Step 2 **Identify Sources** You need to find information about your topic. Relevant sources are books, magazine articles, or websites.

Step 3 **Find and Record Information** Use sources to find information about what types of objects in your home can be recycled. Write down each source.

Step 4 **Organize and Combine Information** Categorize the items. You may group items together that are paper, plastic, or metal. Be sure you have information about each kind of recyclable object.

Step 5 **Create and Present** Create your recycling chart. Draw an example of an item from the chart. Share your chart with the class.

Paper	Plastic	Metal

CHECK IN 1 2 3 4

A Call to Compost

? **How does the author use headings to organize "A Call to Compost"?**

COLLABORATE

Talk About It Look back at pages 430–433. Talk about the way the author organizes the information in the article.

Cite Text Evidence In the boxes below, list the heads that the author uses to organize the article. Then tell what each section is about.

Make Inferences

Why do you think the author included the chart on page 433? How does this chart help the reader?

Heads	What this Section is About
Chart Head	What this Chart is About

Write The author uses headings because _____

_____

CHECK IN 1 2 3 4

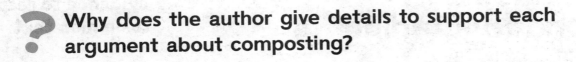

? **Why does the author give details to support each argument about composting?**

Quick Tip

Think about how the author supports each opinion. You can underline supporting evidence, or details, to help you explain each opinion.

Talk About It Reread pages 431-432. Talk about the reasons the author gives to support each argument.

Cite Text Evidence In the boxes below, list three reasons the author gives to support each argument.

Composting Should Be a Law	Composting Should Be a Choice

Write The author gives details for both arguments because

_____

_____

GaryAlvis/iStock/Getty Images

Respond to Reading

Talk about the prompt below. Use your notes and text evidence to support your ideas.

What opinion about a composting law has more convincing reasons and supporting evidence?

_____

_____

_____

_____

_____

_____

CHECK IN 1 2 3 4

Should Students Wear Uniforms?

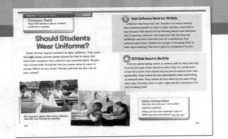

Literature Anthology: pages 434–435

Yes! School Uniforms Work for All Kids

Uniforms help keep kids safe. Teachers can easily identify their students outside of class. In class, teachers want kids to stay focused. Kids should not be thinking about what everyone else is wearing. Uniforms also make kids feel like they are united on one team. Kids feel part of a community. And uniforms save kids the trouble of choosing what to wear each morning. This rule is good for everyone at school.

Reread the page. **Circle** how uniforms help keep kids safe. **Underline** why uniforms help kids learn in school.

Draw a box around another good reason for school uniforms. How can uniforms help kids get ready for school?

_____

_____

_____

COLLABORATE

Identify the author's opinion. Discuss the evidence that supports the opinion. Use vocabulary from the selection.

Paul Bradbury/age footstock

No! Kids Need to Be Kids

Kids are active during school. A uniform will not help kids stay focused. Kids pay better attention when they are comfortable in normal clothes. Kids should also be able to express their own personality. They cannot do that wearing the exact same thing as everyone else. They cannot do that wearing the same thing every day. Choosing what to wear helps kids be themselves. It is part of being a kid.

Reread the page. Does the author believe uniforms help kids concentrate, or focus, on learning?

_____

_____

_____

Underline evidence that supports your answer.

How can wearing a uniform stop kids from expressing their personality?

_____

_____

COLLABORATE

Discuss the evidence that supports each author's opinion. Use vocabulary from the selection.

CHECK IN 1 2 3 4

Author's Opinion

An author's opinion is something the author believes to be true, but others may not think is true. Authors use evidence to try to persuade, or convince, readers to agree with their opinion.

 FIND TEXT EVIDENCE

Reread the opinions on pages 79–80. There are two opinions about school uniforms. Identify the opinion you think is stronger, or more convincing.

_____

_____

Your Turn What evidence makes you believe the opinion is more convincing, or stronger, than the other?

_____

_____

Think about how to convince readers to believe, or agree with, your opinion. When you write an opinion essay, choose the strongest, most convincing facts and details that support what you believe.

MAKE CONNECTIONS

? **What have you learned from the selections you read and the poem about why rules are important?**

COLLABORATE

Talk About It Read the poem "At Table" below. Then talk about how manners are rules for our families.

Cite Text Evidence **Circle** the parts in the poem that tell something a person with good manners would not do.

Write The selections I read and the poem show me that

rules are important because _____

_____

_____

"At Table" from *More Goops and How Not to Be Them*

Why is it Goops must always wish
To touch *each* apple on the dish?
Why do they never neatly fold
Their napkins until they are told?

Why do they play with food, and bite
Such awful mouthfuls? Is it right?
Why do they tilt back in their chairs?
Because they're Goops! So no one cares!

— Gelett Burgess

CHECK IN 1 > 2 > 3 > 4

Create a Book of Rules

Think about the rules you read about. Think about why people believe these rules are important. How can these rules benefit our lives? Write a picture book of important rules you learned about.

1. Look at your Build Knowledge notes in your reader's notebook.

2. In your book of rules, write and illustrate three rules. They may be rules for your home, school, or town. Give one or two reasons why you believe each is important to follow. Support your reasons with evidence from the texts you read.

3. Include some of the new words you learned. Remember to use evidence from three texts to support your ideas.

Think about what you learned in this text set. Fill in the bars on page 63.

Think about what you already know. Fill in the bars. Now let's get started!

Key

1 =	I do not understand.
2 =	I understand but need more practice.
3 =	I understand.
4 =	I understand and can teach someone.

What I Know Now

I can write an opinion essay.

1 > 2 > 3 > 4

I can combine information from two sources.

1 > 2 > 3 > 4

STOP You will come back to the next page later.

Think about what you learned. Fill in the bars. The more you write, the more you'll improve.

What I Learned

I can write an opinion essay.

1 > 2 > 3 > 4

I can combine information from two sources.

1 > 2 > 3 > 4

WRITE TO SOURCES

You will answer an opinion prompt using sources and a rubric.

ANALYZE THE RUBRIC

A rubric tells you what to include in your writing.

Purpose, Focus, and Organization

Read the second bullet. What does the writing support?

_____

_____

Read the fifth bullet. **Underline** what the essay includes.

Evidence and Elaboration

Read the second bullet. **Draw a box** around what relevant evidence means. **Circle** where it comes from.

Opinion Writing Rubric

Purpose, Focus, and Organization • Score 4

- Stays focused on purpose, audience, and task
- **States an opinion that is supported in each part of the essay**
- Connects ideas with transitional words
- Presents ideas in a logical order
- Begins with an introduction and ends with a conclusion that sums up the opinion

Evidence and Elaboration • Score 4

- Supports the opinion with facts and details
- Includes relevant evidence, or supporting details, from the sources
- Uses different types of details that show understanding of the topic
- Expresses ideas clearly with precise language
- Uses academic vocabulary to explain the topic
- Has different sentence types and lengths

Turn to page 126 for the complete Opinion Writing Rubric.

Opinion Statement

State Your Opinion An opinion is what the writer thinks or believes about a topic. Clearly state your opinion in the beginning of your essay. Read the introduction below. The opinion statement is highlighted.

> Purpose
>
> The purpose of an opinion essay is to persuade readers to think a certain way, or to agree with an opinion. It has reasons to agree with the writer's opinion.

> Everyone in a family can be super busy with school or jobs. It's important that families work as a team. Kids need to do their part at home. **Kids should not get paid when they help with household chores.**

What is the writer's opinion about kids doing chores?

_____

_____

Supporting Details Writers use details to support their opinion. Supporting details, or relevant evidence, help the reader understand what the writer thinks about a topic.

Reread the paragraph above. **Underline** two details that support the writer's opinion.

ANALYZE THE STUDENT MODEL

Paragraph 1

What details in the introduction got you interested in the topic?

_____

_____

_____

Paragraph 2

Circle the reason why Julie thinks kids should do chores for free.

Underline examples Julie gives of lessons kids learn.

Julie explains why she disagrees with the author of "No Pay, No Chores." **Draw a box** around these two sentences.

Student Model: Opinion Essay

Julie responded to the writing prompt: _Write an opinion essay that explains whether kids should get paid for doing chores._ Read Julie's essay below.

> 1   Everyone in a family can be super busy with school or jobs. It's important that families work as a team. Kids need to do their part at home. Kids should not get paid when they help with household chores.
>
> 2   Kids should do chores for free because it is the right thing to do. The author of "Family Helpers" explains that doing chores for this reason "teaches lessons more valuable than money." Kids learn about being considerate. Doing chores teaches them to think about the needs of other family members. The author of "No Pay, No Chores" says kids should be paid for chores. And then they will learn that hard work is rewarded. But kids can feel rewarded in ways other than money. A thank-you is reward enough when you do the right thing.

3 Parents can teach kids about money with an allowance. The author of "No Pay, No Chores" might believe that kids learn the value of money when they work for money. I disagree. The other author explains how an allowance can help kids "learn to buy what they need before what they want." An expert in childcare named Doctor Spock agrees that kids can learn to use money with an allowance.

4 Adult family members do work around the house and are not paid for it. Kids should remember this before they ask for money to pick up after play or to make their beds. Kids should not get paid for being helpful and considerate to their family members.

Paragraph 3

How can parents teach kids about money without paying for chores?

_____

_____

Underline evidence Julie uses to support this reason.

Paragraph 4

Look back at the highlighted text in paragraph 1. Draw a box around the sentence in the conclusion that tells Julie's opinion in a new way.

Apply the Rubric

With a partner, use the rubric on page 86 to discuss why Julie scored 10 points on her essay.

Analyze the Prompt

Writing Prompt

Write an opinion essay that explains whether second graders should volunteer in the community.

Purpose, Audience, and Task Reread the writing prompt. What is your purpose for writing? My purpose is to _____

_____

Who will your audience be? My audience will be _____

_____

What type of writing is the prompt asking for? _____

_____

Set a Purpose for Reading Sources Asking questions about kids volunteering will help you figure out your purpose for reading. Write a question before reading the passage set.

_____

_____

Read the following passage set.

Future Volunteers

1   Volunteering can teach kids many things, such as teamwork and being a responsible citizen. But second graders are too busy and too young to be volunteers. Let children practice working in groups in the classroom. Family members can teach them the value of helping others.

2   **Second graders have full days already**. At school, kids study from morning into the afternoon. After school, many kids do organized activities. They play sports or learn about the arts. Then they have chores and homework to do at home. When do kids get free time to play? Playtime is good for children. It's a time for them to try new things and explore their interests.

3   Kids aren't ready to contribute, or help. Adults must teach and supervise young volunteers. This takes away time the adults have to do important work. Kids should first learn about the needs of their community. Then they will be ready to make a difference in the future.

OPINION ESSAY

FIND TEXT EVIDENCE 🔍

Paragraph 1

Draw a box around the opinion statement. Does the author think second graders should be volunteers?

_____

_____

_____

Paragraph 2

Read the highlighted reason. **Underline** details that describe why kids are too busy to be volunteers.

Paragraph 3

Circle details that support the reason that kids are not ready to help.

📝 **Take Notes** Paraphrase the author's opinion and give examples of supporting details.

WRITING

Paragraph 4

Draw a box around what kids do in a book drive. What does the author want readers to think about by describing a book drive?

_____

_____

Paragraph 5

Underline how kids can help at an animal shelter.

Circle what kids can do in their school community. What is an example of an event where kids help?

_____

_____

Kids Volunteer

4   Imagine helping in a book drive. Families donate their old books to you and your classmates. The books are for young readers. Your team of volunteers brings the books to kindergartners. The faces of the girls and boys light up with smiles. This gives you a great feeling. A book drive is just one of many ways that kids can help their community.

5   What are other ways to volunteer? Some animal shelters allow school children to visit. Kids bring supplies for the shelter, such as old blankets. They also help care for the animals. Often, school communities help raise money for an organization or good cause. Kids help at events called fundraisers. One example is called a walkathon. People pledge donations, or money, for kids and family members to walk for charity.

6 **Young volunteers benefit when they help others.** Kids build skills when they work in groups to reach a goal. They also build friendships. Volunteering can also be an enjoyable time for families to spend together. Most importantly, volunteers learn about other people and the value of giving.

7 Kids are not too young to donate their time and energy. There are plenty of groups that welcome their help. Kids gain valuable experience. They also make a difference in the community.

Students volunteer at animal shelters.

Children who volunteer:

- help people
- learn about others
- build friendships
- learn new skills
- build confidence

FIND TEXT EVIDENCE

Paragraph 6

A reason for the opinion is highlighted. **Circle** an example of how kids benefit.

What does the author feel is the most important benefit?

_____

_____

_____

Paragraph 7

Underline a detail that explains why kids are not too young to volunteer.

Bulleted List

Draw a box around a benefit that the author does not include in paragraph 6.

Take Notes Paraphrase the opinion and give examples of supporting details.

My Goal I can combine information from two sources.

TAKE NOTES

Read the writing prompt below. Use the sources, your notes, and the graphic organizer to plan a response.

Writing Prompt *Write an opinion essay that explains whether second graders should volunteer in the community.*

Combine Information

Review the relevant evidence recorded from each source. How does the information support your opinion? Discuss your ideas with a partner.

CHECK IN 1 2 3 4

Plan: Organize Ideas

Opinion	Supporting Reasons
Second graders should/should not volunteer in the community.	One reason is . . .

Relevant Evidence	
Source 1	**Source 2**

Draft: Relevant Evidence

Supporting Details Use different types of details from the sources, such as quotations and examples. Do not include unimportant details that do not support your opinion. Read part of a draft of Julie's essay below.

> Kids should do chores for free because it is the right thing to do. The author of "Family Helpers" explains that doing chores for this reason "teaches lessons more valuable than money." Kids learn about being considerate. It's not fun to wipe off a dirty table.

Quick Tip

Include relevant evidence, or supporting details, from all the sources. If you disagree with an author's opinion or claim about the topic, you can explain to your readers why.

Circle the name of the source. **Underline** the relevant evidence Julie uses from the source. **Cross out** the unimportant detail. Why is this detail not relevant evidence?

_____

_____

 Use your graphic organizer to write your draft. Be sure to include relevant evidence and refer to, or name, the sources. Before you start writing, review the rubric on page 86.

CHECK IN 1 2 3 4

Revise: Peer Conferences

Review a Draft Listen carefully as a partner reads his or her work aloud. Say what you like about the draft. Use these sentence starters to talk about your partner's draft.

I like the evidence you used to support your opinion…
I have a question about…
I think you can add details about…

Write one of the suggestions from your partner that you will use in your revision.

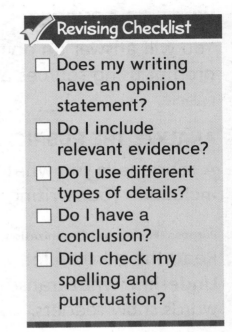

Revising Checklist

☐ Does my writing have an opinion statement?
☐ Do I include relevant evidence?
☐ Do I use different types of details?
☐ Do I have a conclusion?
☐ Did I check my spelling and punctuation?

Revision Use the Revising Checklist to help you figure out what text you may need to move, elaborate on, or delete. When you finish writing your final draft, use the full rubric on page 126 to score your essay.

Next, you'll write an opinion essay on a new topic.

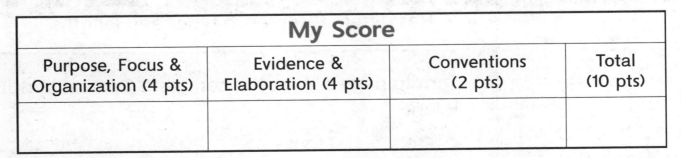

My Score			
Purpose, Focus & Organization (4 pts)	Evidence & Elaboration (4 pts)	Conventions (2 pts)	Total (10 pts)

WRITE TO SOURCES

You will answer an opinion prompt using sources and a rubric.

ANALYZE THE RUBRIC

A rubric tells you what to include in your writing.

Purpose, Focus, and Organization

Read the third bullet. **Underline** what transitional words show readers.

Evidence and Elaboration

Read the third bullet. **Circle** what details in your essay will show readers.

Read the fourth bullet. How can you express ideas clearly?

_____

_____

_____

Opinion Writing Rubric

Purpose, Focus, and Organization • Score 4
• Stays focused on purpose, audience, and task
• States an opinion that is supported in each part of the essay
• **Connects ideas with transitional words**
• Presents ideas in a logical order
• Begins with an introduction and ends with a conclusion that sums up the opinion

Evidence and Elaboration • Score 4
• Supports the opinion with facts and details
• Includes relevant evidence, or supporting details, from the sources
• Uses different types of details that show understanding of the topic
• Expresses ideas clearly with precise language
• Uses academic vocabulary to explain the topic
• Has different sentence types and lengths

Turn to page 126 for the complete Opinion Writing Rubric.

Transitional Words

Connect Ideas Transitional words show how ideas are connected. For example, *because* can show a cause or reason why something is true. Read the paragraph below. The writer uses words that help readers understand how the ideas in the paragraph are connected.

> People will continue to ride bikes **because** it's such great exercise. Also, riding a bike can save grown-ups money. In addition, it is a fun way to get around.

Why does the writer believe people will continue to ride bikes?

_____

_____

Reread the paragraph above. **Circle** the words that show other reasons why people will continue to ride bikes. **Underline** these reasons.

Valentain Jevee/Shutterstock

ANALYZE THE STUDENT MODEL

Paragraph 1

Ric's opinion is highlighted. What will his essay explain, or support?

_____

_____

_____

Paragraph 2

What will the law help people understand? **Underline** Ric's first reason.

Paragraph 3

Ric supports his reason that the law will protect riders. **Circle** relevant evidence from "Helmets Save Lives." **Draw a box** around the quotation from "No Bike Helmet Law."

Student Model: Opinion Essay

Ric responded to the writing prompt: _Write an opinion essay that explains whether there should be a law to make bike riders wear helmets._ Read Ric's essay below.

1 Bike riding is fun with family and friends. Some adults also bike to jobs. But riding a bike can be dangerous. We need a law that makes bike riders wear helmets.

2 The law will help people understand the dangers of riding a bike. The author of "Helmets Save Lives" points out that rocks and wet leaves can be "hazards" on the road. Riders can fall even if they follow safety rules.

3 Helmets can protect riders from getting badly hurt. The author of "Helmets Save Lives" tells how accidents cause injuries, and a helmet can make the injuries less serious. The author of "No Bike Helmet Law" tells us that "bike helmets can prevent head injuries." It is too much of a risk to ride without a helmet.

4   In "No Bike Helmet Law," the author says a helmet law will make people bike less. I disagree! People will continue to ride bikes because it's such great exercise. Also, riding a bike can save grown-ups money. In addition, it is a fun way to get around. The author in favor of the law points out that helmets are light and comfortable. They don't bother riders. With the law, "wearing a helmet will become a habit." No one will think twice about it.

5   We make laws to keep us safe. Even the author against the law admits, "Everyone should wear a helmet when they bike." A law for bike helmets makes sense. It will help bike riders get around on their bikes safely.

Paragraph 4
What idea about a helmet law does Ric disagree with?

_____

_____

Circle the reference to the source Ric disagrees with.

Underline a quotation that helps explain why the law will not be a problem.

Paragraph 5
Draw a box around two sentences in the conclusion that restate Ric's opinion.

Apply the Rubric

With a partner, use the rubric on page 98 to discuss why Ric scored 10 points on his essay.

Analyze the Prompt

Writing Prompt

Write an essay that explains your opinion about whether children should have limits on "screen time."

Purpose, Audience, and Task Reread the writing prompt. What is your purpose for writing? My purpose is to _____

_____

Who will your audience be? My audience will be _____

_____

What type of writing is the prompt asking for? _____

_____

Set a Purpose for Reading Sources Asking questions about the use of electronic devices will help you understand what you want to learn from the passages. Before you read the passage set, write a question here.

_____

_____

Read the following passage set.

SMART SCREEN TIME

1   We can't stop kids from playing video games or watching television. They stare at screens for hours every day. But we can help them be smarter users of digital media. Let's help our kids understand that devices are for fun *and* learning.

2   **Share screen time with kids.** Read trusted sources that tell about the best apps and games for kids. Play these video games together. Watch educational programs together. Always encourage kids to ask questions and talk about what they watch.

3   Discuss times to take a break from devices. Help kids understand that certain occasions are for sharing with family and friends.

4   Let's help kids use devices safely and with respect for others. Screen time can be for learning as well as a time to bring families together.

wavebreakmedia/Shutterstock

OPINION ESSAY

FIND TEXT EVIDENCE

Paragraph 1
Underline why the author does not think we can limit screen time. What is the author's opinion?

_____

_____

_____

Paragraph 2
Read the highlighted sentence. **Draw a box** around an example of sharing screen time with kids.

Paragraph 3
Circle the detail that tells what the author wants kids to understand.

Take Notes Paraphrase the opinion of the source and give examples of supporting details.

FIND TEXT EVIDENCE

Paragraph 5

Draw a box around what the author thinks adults need to limit. Why does the author have this opinion?

_____

_____

Paragraph 6

A reason is highlighted. **Underline** the details that tell what kids learn from play with friends. **Circle** what this time without screens does for kids.

Paragraph 7

What is the second reason to limit screen time?

_____

_____

No More Screen Time

5 A computer is a digital tool. Kids use it to learn about the world. They use it to write and draw—to express ideas. Outside of the classroom is a different story. Kids waste their free time glued to games, videos, and TV shows. We need to limit their screen time. Kids need time for activities that help them learn and grow.

6 **First, kids need to spend more time with friends.** Boys and girls learn new ideas from their friends. During playtime, they also learn about sharing. In addition, time without screens challenges kids to use their imagination and find creative ways to have fun.

7 Second, kids need more time to exercise. Being active is important for good health. Athletics can also teach valuable lessons. Kids learn about teamwork. They learn the importance of sportsmanship.

Kids have fun learning to play soccer.

8   Last, kids need time for sleep. They need 8–12 hours each day. A good night's rest makes everyone a better learner. Kids should never watch TV or use a device before bedtime. This is a rule that everyone can follow. Screen time before bed can be bad for a person's sleep.

9   Kids use computers for learning at school. After homework, there's no time to waste in front of a screen. Time away from screens will help kids learn and grow.

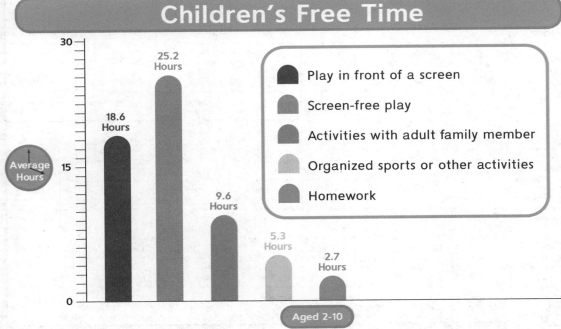

Children's Free Time

Average Hours

- Play in front of a screen — 18.6 Hours
- Screen-free play — 25.2 Hours
- Activities with adult family member — 9.6 Hours
- Organized sports or other activities — 5.3 Hours
- Homework — 2.7 Hours

Aged 2-10

OPINION ESSAY

FIND TEXT EVIDENCE

Paragraph 8

Circle two facts about the sleep kids need.

Underline why the author thinks people should avoid screen time before bedtime.

Chart

Compare the number of hours kids spend in front of a screen with the time they spend doing homework and organized activities.

_____

_____

_____

Take Notes Paraphrase the opinion and give examples of supporting details.

My Goal I can combine information from two sources.

TAKE NOTES

Read the writing prompt below. Use the sources, your notes, and the graphic organizer to plan a response.

Writing Prompt *Write an essay that explains your opinion about whether children should have limits on "screen time."*

Combine Information

Review the relevant evidence recorded from each source. How does the information support your opinion? Discuss your ideas with a partner.

CHECK IN 1 2 3 4

Plan: Organize Ideas

Opinion	Supporting Reasons
We should/should not have a limit on screen time.	One reason is . . .

Relevant Evidence

Source 1	Source 2

Draft: Supporting Reason

Paragraphs You may tell about a reason in a paragraph. Use relevant evidence to explain the reason in detail. Read paragraph 3 from Ric's essay. The reason is highlighted.

> **Helmets can protect riders from getting badly hurt.** The author of "Helmets Save Lives" tells how accidents cause injuries, and a helmet can make the injuries less serious. The author of "No Bike Helmet Law" tells us that "bike helmets can prevent head injuries." It is too much of a risk to ride without a helmet.

Underline the details from the sources Ric uses to support the reason. **Circle** Ric's concluding statement.

Use your graphic organizer to organize each part of your essay, including an introduction and a conclusion. Then write your draft in your writer's notebook. Before you start writing, review the rubric on page 98.

Fat Camera/E+/Getty Images

CHECK IN 1 2 3 4

Revise: Peer Conferences

Review a Draft Listen carefully as a partner reads his or her work aloud. Say what you like about the draft. Use these sentence starters to talk about your partner's draft.

I like the evidence you used to support the reason...
I have a question about...
I think you can add details about...

Write one of the suggestions from your partner that you will use in your revision.

Turn to page 85. Fill in the bars to show what you learned.

Revision Use the Revising Checklist to help you figure out what text you may need to move, elaborate on, or delete. When you finish writing your final draft, use the full rubric on page 126 to score your essay.

My Score			
Purpose, Focus & Organization (4 pts)	Evidence & Elaboration (4 pts)	Conventions (2 pts)	Total (10 pts)

My Goal I can read and understand social studies texts.

TAKE NOTES

Take notes and annotate as you read the passages "George Washington Carver" and "Jacqueline Cochran: American Flier."

Look for the answer to this question: *How can one person's work make a difference to many Americans?*

_____

_____

_____

_____

_____

PASSAGE **1**

BIOGRAPHY

George Washington Carver

When are peanuts more than peanuts? It's when they become milk or even soap. Scientist and teacher George Washington Carver discovered hundreds of uses for peanuts.

Carver was born in the early 1860s on a farm in Missouri. His family was enslaved until 1865 when slavery was abolished, or ended. Carver left home as a boy to find work and go to school.

He had an interest in farming. He attended college. There, Carver studied the science of agriculture. He became head of the agriculture program at Tuskegee Institute in Alabama.

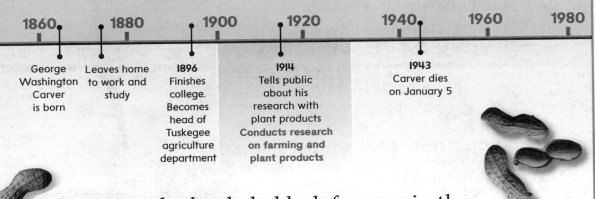

1860	1880	1900	1920	1940	1960	1980

1860
George Washington Carver is born

1880
Leaves home to work and study

1896
Finishes college. Becomes head of Tuskegee agriculture department

1914
Tells public about his research with plant products
Conducts research on farming and plant products

1943
Carver dies on January 5

Carver worked to help black farmers in the South. Cotton had been the main crop for a long time, and that hurt the soil. Carver taught farmers how to take turns growing different crops to help the soil. One year, they would grow peanuts, and the next year sweet potatoes. This rotation helped the soil keep its nutrients so all crops could grow.

To help farmers sell the new crops, he looked for new ways to use them. He found that peanuts could be used to make flour, inks, and dyes, even face cream and medicine. Sweet potatoes could be used to make vinegar, glue, and other products. Farmers made money from these crops.

Carver improved farming and the lives of farmers. He is seen as a hero to many people.

C Squared Studios/Photodisc/Getty Images

TAKE NOTES

_____

_____

_____

_____

_____

_____

_____

_____

_____

_____

_____

_____

PASSAGE 2   **BIOGRAPHY**

JACQUELINE COCHRAN: AMERICAN FLIER

Did you know that sound travels at about 760 miles in an hour? If an aircraft travels faster than that, it makes a loud sonic boom. In 1953, a woman named Jacqueline Cochran became the first woman to fly an aircraft faster than sound. This achievement is just one of many in her exciting life.

Cochran was born in Florida in 1906. When she grew up, she moved to New York City. One day, a friend gave Cochran her first ride in an airplane. From that moment on, Cochran knew that she must fly. She signed up for lessons right away. Soon after that, she began competing in air races around the country.

In 1941, Cochran wanted to help the war effort. The United States had not yet entered what would come to be known as World War II. Cochran offered her flying skills to England. There she began training women to fly planes.

When America entered the war, Cochran returned. She formed a group called the Women Airforce Service Pilots. The women pilots were trained to transport aircraft, soldiers, and supplies. Cochran loved flying and was proud to serve her country. After the war ended, she was awarded the Distinguished Service Medal.

Jacqueline Cochran died in 1980. She had set more flying records than any other pilot in the world.

Jacqueline Cochran helped American women to become pilots.

TAKE NOTES

Compare the Passages

Talk About It Reread your notes from "George Washington Carver" and "Jacqueline Cochran: American Flier." Talk with a partner about how these two people made a difference in the lives of Americans.

Cite Text Evidence Fill in the chart with details about the important work that each person did.

George Washington Carver

What he did...

↓

How it made a difference...

Jacqueline Cochran

What she did...

↓

How it made a difference...

? **How can one person's work make a difference to many Americans?**

Talk About It Look at the graphic organizer on page 114. Talk about "George Washington Carver" and "Jacqueline Cochran: American Flier." What kind of work did each person do? How did their work affect other people?

Write One person can make a difference by _____

_____

_____

_____

_____

Quick Tip

Use these sentence starters to talk about how each person helped others through their work and actions.

George Washington Carver wanted to help...

He taught farmers...

Jacqueline Cochran loved to...

She helped women...

Combine Information

Why is it important to learn about the contributions of people like George Washington Carver and Jacqueline Cochran? Why do you think they still inspire Americans today?

CHECK IN 1 2 3 4

Role Model Comic Strip

George Washington Carver and Jacqueline Cochran are role models to many people. Who are your role models?

Talk with a partner about a person you admire. Explain why you want to do things like this person. Then, create a comic strip that illustrates why you look up to your role model. Write a caption for each picture.

Quick Tip

Your role model can be a person in your community or someone from history. Before you begin, talk with your partner about what you will draw in each box.

_____ _____ _____

_____ _____ _____

_____ _____ _____

Write a Letter to Your Role Model

Write a letter to your role model. Explain why you appreciate the things this person has done and how he or she inspires you in your life. You can use your work on page 116 to help you with ideas. Remember to include the following:

Heading Write the date at the top of your letter.

Greeting Begin *Dear* and the name of your role model.

Body Write one or two paragraphs that express your ideas to your role model.

Closing Write a closing word or phrase, such as *Sincerely*. Then write your signature.

Quick Tip

Remember to include commas after the greeting and the closing. You may also include your address in the heading of your letter. This shows where the reader can address, or send, a letter back to you.

_____

_____

_____

_____

_____

C Squared Studios/Photodisc/Getty Images

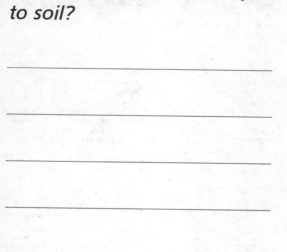

My Goal I can read and understand science texts.

TAKE NOTES

Take notes and annotate as you read the passages "Compost: Food for Your Soil!" and "Spreading the Garden Love."

Look for the answer to these questions: *What is compost? Why do people add compost to soil?*

_____

_____

_____

_____

PASSAGE 1

EXPOSITORY ESSAY

COMPOST: Food for Your Soil!

Don't throw that apple peel away! Recycle it by tossing it into a compost bin!

A compost bin is a place where your food scraps and yard waste decompose. This means the stuff breaks down into smaller and smaller bits called compost.

Putting compost into soil makes the soil richer. It helps keep moisture in. Farmers know that some soils are better than others. They improve their soil by adding compost. This helps them grow better fruits and vegetables. Compost helps flowers grow, too!

Nature composts all the time. Take an autumn walk through a forest. See the leaves falling all around? The dry leaves begin to break apart. Over time, the dry leaf material becomes part of the soil in the forest.

tbkgd)McGraw-Hill Education, (t)Evan Lorne/Shutterstock

The nutrients from the leaves go into the soil and feed the tree and other plants around it.

You may think of soil as just something that gets you dirty when you play outside. But soil is so much more than that. It's a natural resource, just like air and water.

If you picture Earth as an onion with many layers, then soil is the outer layer. It's formed from dead plants, dead animals, and bits of rock that break down over time. When you put compost into soil, you're feeding it. You're making the soil a healthy place for new plants to grow!

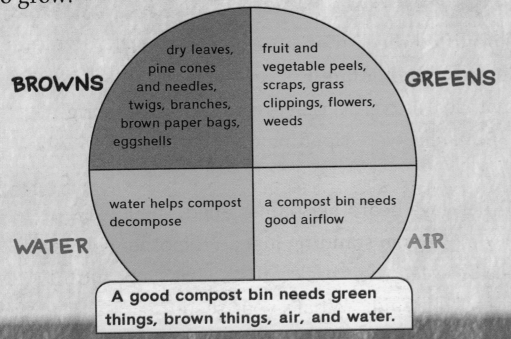

BROWNS
dry leaves, pine cones and needles, twigs, branches, brown paper bags, eggshells

GREENS
fruit and vegetable peels, scraps, grass clippings, flowers, weeds

WATER
water helps compost decompose

AIR
a compost bin needs good airflow

A good compost bin needs green things, brown things, air, and water.

TAKE NOTES

_____

_____

_____

_____

_____

_____

_____

_____

_____

_____

_____

_____

_____

PASSAGE 2 REALISTIC FICTION

Spreading the Garden Love

Jaya lifted the garden hose and let the silvery spray rain down on her family's vegetable garden. The tomato leaves were a rich green and several bright red tomatoes were ripening on the vine, ready to be picked.

When Jaya heard her name called, she looked up to see Mrs. Carson standing just on the other side of the fence between their backyards. "That's a beautiful garden," she said. "What's your secret?"

"There's no secret," Jaya laughed. "We put compost in the soil. It's natural and it helps the plants grow. We don't use any harmful chemicals!"

Mrs. Carson nodded. "Where do you buy this compost?" she asked. "My garden needs some help."

"We don't buy it," Jaya explained. "We make it." She walked over to her family's compost bin. "We put our table scraps in there, along with grass clippings, dry leaves, and eggshells. After a while, everything starts to break down into compost."

"Jaya, three of my gardening friends are coming over later," Mrs. Carson began. "If you're free, would you talk to us about composting? Maybe you could show us how your family composts!"

"I'll ask Mom," Jaya said. "It's funny, because when we spread the compost, we call it 'Spreading the Garden Love!' So I think Mom will be happy for me to spread some garden love to our neighbors!"

Compare the Passages

Talk About It Reread your notes from "Compost: Food for Your Soil!" and "Spreading the Garden Love." Talk with a partner about what compost is and how it helps soil.

Cite Text Evidence Fill in the chart with details from the text.

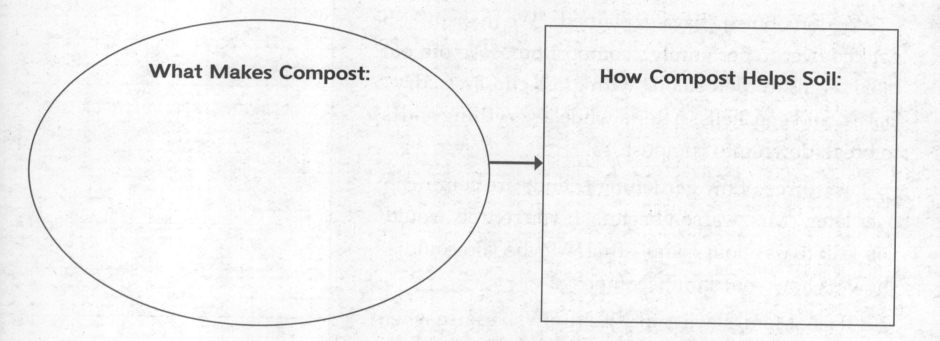

What Makes Compost:

How Compost Helps Soil:

What is compost? Why do people add compost to soil?

COLLABORATE

Talk About It Look at the graphic organizer on page 122. Talk about "Compost: Food for Your Soil!" and "Spreading the Garden Love." What did you learn about compost and soil from these passages? How does compost help soil?

Write People choose to make compost because _____

_____

_____

Compost can help soil _____

_____

_____

Quick Tip

Use these sentence starters to talk about compost.

Compost can be made of...

Compost helps soil by...

Soil that has compost...

Combine Information

Composting has many benefits. What benefits did you learn about from the passages? What other benefits do you think composting has on the environment?

Persuade People to Compost

COLLABORATE

Composting has many benefits. Think about the texts you've read in this unit. Talk about how composting helps people and the environment. Write and draw your ideas in the box.

Quick Tip

Talk about how composting affects:

- Yard waste
- Food scraps
- Soil
- Plants

With a partner, make a poster to persuade people to compost. Show your audience why composting can help them and the environment. Share your poster with the class.

Reflect on Your Learning

Talk About It Reflect on what you learned in this unit. Then talk with a partner about how you did.

I am really proud of how I can _____

_____

_____

_____

_____

Share a goal you have with a partner.

Something I need to work more on is _____

_____

_____

_____

_____

My Goal Set a goal for Unit 6. In your reader's notebook, write about what you can do to get there.

Opinion Writing Rubric

Score	Purpose, Focus, and Organization (4-point Rubric)	Evidence and Elaboration (4-point Rubric)	Conventions of Standard English (2-point Rubric)
4	• Stays focused on purpose, audience, and task • States an opinion that is supported in each part of the essay • Connects ideas with transitional words • Presents ideas in a logical order • Begins with an introduction and ends with a conclusion that sums up the opinion	• Supports the opinion with facts and details • Includes relevant evidence, or supporting details, from the sources • Uses different types of details that show understanding of the topic • Expresses ideas clearly with precise language • Uses academic vocabulary to explain the topic • Has different sentence types and lengths	

Score	Purpose, Focus, and Organization (4-point Rubric)	Evidence and Elaboration (4-point Rubric)	Conventions of Standard English (2-point Rubric)
3	• Stays mostly focused on purpose, audience, and task • States an opinion that is supported in some parts of the essay • Connects ideas with some transitional words • Presents ideas in a logical order • Begins with an introduction and ends with a conclusion that sums up the opinion	• Supports the opinion with facts and details • Includes relevant evidence, or supporting details, from some sources • Uses an acceptable amount of different types of details that show understanding of the topic • Expresses ideas with some precise language • Uses some academic vocabulary to explain the topic • Has some different sentence types and lengths	

Opinion Writing Rubric

Score	Purpose, Focus, and Organization (4-point Rubric)	Evidence and Elaboration (4-point Rubric)	Conventions of Standard English (2-point Rubric)
2	• Does not stay focused on purpose, audience, and task • States an opinion that is not supported in the essay • Connects ideas with few transitional words • Does not present ideas in a logical order • Does not have an introduction and/or conclusion	• Supports the opinion with weak facts and details • Includes weak evidence, or supporting details, from few sources • Uses an acceptable amount of different types of details that show understanding of the topic • Expresses ideas with little use of precise language • Uses few academic vocabulary to explain the topic • Has little variety of sentence types and lengths	• Shows understanding of basic grammar and usage conventions • Has some minor errors in word usage, but there is not a pattern of mistakes • Has acceptable usage of punctuation, capitalization, and spelling

Score	Purpose, Focus, and Organization (4-point Rubric)	Evidence and Elaboration (4-point Rubric)	Conventions of Standard English (2-point Rubric)
1	• Does not stay focused on purpose, audience, and task • Does not state an opinion clearly • Has unrelated ideas and is confusing and unclear • Has few or no transitional words • Is too brief, or short, to show focus or organization	• Shows little or no support for opinion • Includes little to no use of sources, facts, or details • Expresses ideas that are confusing • Uses few content words or academic vocabulary that is not appropriate to the audience and purpose • Has only short, simple sentences	• Shows some understanding of basic grammar and usage conventions • Has many errors in word usage • Has little or no use of punctuation, capitalization • Has incomplete sentences and many spelling errors
0			• Shows a lack of understanding of grammar and usage conventions • Has many errors that confuse the reader